God's Presence in the Present

God's Presence in the Present

Contemplative Prayer and the Healing Process

Michael Hoffner

God's Presence in the Present: Contemplative Prayer and the
Healing Process

Dedication

This book is dedicated to all those living with mental illness and addiction. Especially those currently struggling to find peace and serenity within themselves and their world. May these words be offered up as testimony that you are not forgotten.

Acknowledgments

Thank you to my parents, Ellen and David Hoffner. You have been a constant source of strength and encouragement for me on my journey and I would not be here without you. Your help as my editors and review readers on this book has helped make this book what it is today. I love you.

To my wife, Christine, thank you for your love and encouragement. I am only able to do what I do because I know you are there supporting me. Your courage and strength is an inspiration for all that are lucky enough to witness it.

Jim Barker, my Spiritual Director and friend. Thank you for your continued guidance and support on my spiritual journey.

Sister Jean Peter Olsen, O.P. Thank you for our spirituality sessions and helping guide me as I moved deeper into my prayer life. Thank you for your insight and feedback during the early stages of the writing process, it truly helped shape the content of this book. Most importantly, thank you for being present and sharing in the presence of God with me, it was truly sacred time on holy ground.

To the many hands and hearts at Hope House Ministries, especially my Godmother Patty Griffin.

A special thank you to Fr. Francis Pizzarelli, for your wisdom and direction throughout the last 12 years of my life. You are a shining example of what it means to live a life following Jesus. Your work reaching out to the outcast and marginalized is an inspiration for all. Thank you for adding your touch to this book with your foreword.

Table of Contents

A Message from the Author

It is my prayer that through God's grace I can use the following pages to share the process through which I have come to know the depth of God's love for us and to find healing. This book is by no means an autobiography, however, everything I express in this book has been written because I know it to be true from my own experiences. I do want to briefly share a piece of my story to help show where I have been and to help give witness to the awesome power of God's love for us.

On Ash Wednesday 2002, at the age of 22, I was sitting in the waiting area of Mercy Medical Center on Long Island with my mother and a dear friend of mine. I was waiting to go through my first intake process in the hopes of addressing my anxiety, depression and drug addiction. This would be the start of a four-year journey in and out of different inpatient psychiatric hospitals and drug rehab centers, numerous outpatient programs for mental health and addiction and an overdose that left me in the ICU for three days.

On May 31, 2006, I met Fr. Francis Pizzarelli and walked through the doors of Hope House Ministries. Thus began my journey back to healing. I have since gone back to school and received my Master in Social Work and in 2015 opened the Community Growth Center, a non-profit holistic health center for self-discovery and contemplative healing. The specific details surrounding my past are not significant to this book other than to give thanks to God, for I was lost and now I am found.

It is my belief that our healing requires a holistic approach, healing the mind, body and spirit. Embracing the practice of Contemplative Prayer and the process discussed in this book, with the guidance and support from trained spiritual directors and counselors I have been able to lean into all three areas of my being (mind, body, spirit). At times in the past I have also used medication to help support my healing process. When we break a bone we use a cast to assist our recovery, helping us to eventually advance to physical therapy in order to fully heal. Similarly, medication, when part of a larger treatment plan, can serve as a valuable support, helping to move us forward so that we may fully heal. My journey, and the process discussed in this book has allowed me to find true healing and "the peace that surpasses all understanding" (Philippians 4:7 ESV).

This book is for all those that have felt lost or incomplete. I pray that it helps you find your way back home.

Sincerely,
Michael Hoffner, LMSW

Foreword

God's Presence in the Present by Michael Hoffner
is a poignant reminder of the real challenges of
living in a world that hovers in darkness.

The pages that follow are filled with pain,
suffering, insight and human transformation.
The author reminds us very vividly of how our
human disconnect and discontent are connected.
But also reminds us of the power of prayer and
the awareness of the present moment. He
challenges us to stay focused in the present, as
we begin to heal.

God's Presence in the Present is a powerful story of
finding one's way home—reminding all of us
who have ever felt lost or incomplete that
homecoming is possible for everyone.

This is a story about one's journey back to God—
and the importance of the body-mind spirit

connection. It is an invitation to walk out of the darkness into the light. It is a grace-filled opportunity to awaken the God who lives within every soul.

Hopefully reading this book will awaken within every reader the peace we seek to find in God's presence. May this peace empower you to realize all of your untapped potential and possibilities and learn how to leave the world better than when you found it.

May this "coming home" lead you to a new awakening and freedom where hope will always be the anthem of your soul!

The author is living proof that miracles do happen; that change and transformation are possible and homecoming and healing are real.

Say yes to the invitation, say yes to this life-changing adventure. Begin your awakening!

Fr. Francis Pizzarelli, SMM, LCSW-R, ACSW, DCSW
Founder/CEO
Hope House Ministries
May 6, 2018

Introduction

O ur journey to connecting with God's presence in the present moment is not a process of discovering something new, but rather an acknowledgment and awareness of something that was always there. It is like the air we breathe. How often do you stop to acknowledge the air that surrounds you? Our life is sustained by breathing in and out but how often do you stop to remind yourself of this? Do you ever just think: "I am grateful for the fact that I have air to breathe today?" God's presence is like the air that surrounds us. It is always there yet we often forget to remain aware and grateful for its presence.

I invite you to try this exercise, hold your breath for 15 seconds. Quickly you are reminded of your need for the air that surrounds you. With your first breath after just 15 seconds you are probably feeling more grateful than usual for the fact that the air was there for you to breathe. You did not have to discover air, you simply had to remember what was and is always there. It was a returning back to something that never left. As soon as you remembered to breathe again, your breath and the air were immediately back in sync. With that disconnect and subsequent reconnection, you were reminded of your need for the air and a deeper appreciation and sense of gratitude arose for your breath. This is the same process we experience when uniting with God in the present moment. With each disconnect we endure that is followed by a reconnection, our awareness and appreciation for God grows deeper.

What makes God an all loving and all forgiving God is that just like the air that surrounds us, as soon as we seek His presence, He is there waiting for us. For that is where He has been the whole time, "waiting for us." God never left us and will never leave us. We however often drift away from God. I recall a poster I once saw that read: "If you feel far away from God, guess who moved?" The answer is always us.

To experience the presence of God in the present moment is to know that God fully exists in all things and in all places, including in us. God is not more present inside the church walls than He is at our job, on a city street or in nature. God is not more present on Christmas Day than He is every other day of the year. So what happens at church or on Christmas Day that makes it seem as if God is more present? What changes is our awareness of His presence. We are suddenly reminded about something that was always there, yet too often overlooked. God did not increase His presence, we increased our awareness.

What exactly are we referring to when we use the term "present moment?" The present moment is not just a measurement of time, it is an awareness of what is. Bringing our awareness to the present moment means recognizing what is physically happening around us, what thoughts we are thinking, what emotions we are feeling, what actions we are doing and the relationship between these elements. Within the present moment and from this state of awareness, we are able to know ourselves and our world at a deeper level.

However, there is something deeper than just being aware of what you are thinking, feeling or doing. It is being aware of God's presence within you and within what you are doing. The presence within the present. The action we are doing is made holy by our recognition of God's presence within it. Being aware of the present moment is a bridge to the divine. When we connect to the presence of God within the present moment the present moment becomes truly sacred space.[1] The bridge we walk connecting the present moment and God's presence is Contemplative Prayer. When we walk this bridge we begin to recognize that everywhere we go and everything we do is taking place on holy ground.

Being aware of the present moment is the foundation for allowing us to connect with God in a deeper, more personal way. However, we must actively seek Him within the present moment. Simply being in the present moment does not mean we are automatically aware of the presence of God. The present moment opens up a doorway to the presence of God, however we must set the intention to walk through that doorway.

As humans, we often become disconnected from ourselves and from the present moment. Our basic disconnect from ourselves means that we are unaware of our thinking, out of touch with our emotions and not conscious of the motives behind our actions. Being disconnected from ourselves keeps us disconnected from the present moment and ultimately disconnected from God's presence. For many people, the journey to the presence of God begins when the pain and discomfort of being disconnected from ourselves grows deep enough that a sense of discontentment sets in. This discontent opens our heart to wonder, "Is there a better way?" This "better way" as explored in this book, leads us to the presence of God. This journey is more about unlearning old ways than it is about learning anything new. It requires shedding parts of who we have become as opposed to becoming someone new.

Connecting with the presence of God is both a personal practice and a grace bestowed upon us. We are responsible for the practice, God brings His grace. Our practice prepares us to receive God more deeply. God's grace is revealed because God wants nothing more than to share His love with us. He is just waiting for us to be open and willing to receive Him. Connecting with God's presence is a process. We don't open ourselves all at once, it usually happens slowly over time, including times when we have to re-do it after we have taken our will back.

It is the practice of exposing our fears, insecurities and pain to the light of our consciousness and the light of Christ. It is removing the illusion of power and control that our thoughts and emotions have over us and opening our hearts to the mystery and presence of God. We sit in stillness, with no notion of "waiting for something" for the "something" is always there. It is the presence of God. It is the practice of being present to His presence.

Twelve-step programs have a saying: "You are only as sick as your secrets." We must be courageous enough to lean into and identify what we are feeling and embrace the pain we are holding on to. When we don't, these "secrets" poison our way of thinking, feeling and behaving.

We can't be afraid to directly address our fears, insecurities and pain. We must own the fact that sometimes we feel jealous, angry, embarrassed, prideful, etc. Acknowledging our shadow areas, the dark parts of us that we keep hidden from the light, doesn't make us bad or weak people. It makes us human. We need to stop being afraid of being human. Our fear of looking at our shadows and instead only seeing our "pretty side" prevents us from moving towards our divine nature.

Our fear of embracing our humanity cuts us off from an awareness of our divinity. Jesus was fully human and fully divine. We often try to skip over our own humanity and try to just connect with the divinity. However, in order to unite our will with His and become "divine," we must be willing to first become "fully human."

To be fully aware of our humanity and our divinity is to be connected to our whole-self. Our whole-self is the "self" that recognizes all the elements of our being (including the areas we still need to grow in) and is aware of our human-nature and God-nature at work within us.

The process explored in this book discusses the steps we take to connect to our whole-self. It outlines the journey of going from discontent to contemplation, from suffering to joyful surrender. By discovering that we are not controlled or defined by our thoughts, emotions or external experiences, we explore how to connect to the present moment and ultimately how to move into the depths of the present which is the presence of God. We surrender into the arms of God and allow God's will to guide and define our life. Through Contemplative Prayer and the uniting of our will with the will of God, we allow God's thoughts to be our thoughts, God's words to be our words and God's actions to be our actions.

Part I

Disconnected and Discontent

I n the following section, I give a general overview of the origin of our disconnection with the whole-self and the discontent that arises as a result. I use common situations and thought patterns to explain my point, but they are in no way an exclusive representation of how one may begin to feel disconnected and discontent. For the time being, it is more important that you keep an open mind and heart, and, as you read, ask yourself if you can relate to feeling "disconnected to yourself and discontent" rather than focusing on if you can relate to the exact examples I provide.

What does it mean to be disconnected and discontent? When I speak of being disconnected with ourselves, it refers to not being honestly aware of "what we are thinking and why we are thinking it," "what we are feeling and why we are feeling it" or "what we are doing and why we are doing it." As well as, unaware of God's presence within all of those things. I use the term "honestly aware" because we will often tell ourselves lies to justify why we are thinking, feeling or doing something. These "lies" or "justifications" push us further from our whole-self. Honest awareness means we know our whole-self, our areas of light and darkness. To be disconnected means to only know a fraction of who we really are.

The term discontent refers to a state of being that is the result of our disconnection with our whole-self. Our failure to know and connect with our whole-self, leaves us feeling incomplete. This sense that we are incomplete leaves us unsatisfied and discontent with our life and with who we are. As a result, we end up in us searching externally for a sense of wholeness.

Projections

When I was growing up, the window in my second floor elementary school classroom looked out onto a large fenced-in grass field, with two baseball fields on opposite ends. From my seat, I had a perfect view of the field in the north-west corner. Staring out the window, my mind created events and projected scenarios that allowed me to imagine hitting the game winning hit in one instance and making a spectacular game-saving catch in the outfield in the next minute. There is something magical about a child's imagination, the ability to create fantasies that bring us joy and wonder.

However, as we get older, our imagination often becomes a series of projections about the future rooted in fear and anxiety more than joy and wonder. It is no longer a daydream about how we are going to save the day. It becomes, "What if something goes wrong today? What if I say the wrong thing? What is everyone going to think about me?" The list of our projected fears is endless. Our mind does not just settle on asking these questions, it projects a world in which the events take place. On both a mental and internally physical level, we experience the impact of these projections as if they are really happening. If our thoughts are left to run wild we create and recreate scenarios in which all of our fears are played out.

As vividly as if it was happening in real time, we can create a situation in which we say the wrong thing and end up looking foolish in front of everyone. We see ourselves turn bright red and start sweating from embarrassment, we see ourselves walking away with our head down and we begin to feel the shame and insecurity attached to this experience. If we continue on this mental projection we can feel the shame and insecurity transform into anger. As a result, we are now filled with anger about a situation that has never happened! If we are completely disconnected, we now launch into a whole series of projections about the things we wish we could say or do to the person that "made us feel embarrassed" and how we would release all of our anger on them. What started as just a thought, when left unchecked, turns into a long series of projections that create a real emotional response.

This emotional response can impact our behaviors in real life. If our thoughts fill us with anger, we are going to look for a way to release that anger. Perhaps we will be less friendly to co-workers or family members, less patient while driving or with the store clerk. Whom we end up taking this emotion out on, and how we release it, is not certain, but what is certain is that without proper awareness, it will be released in an unhealthy way.

Memories

Our experiences as adults are seen and created through the frame of mind and lens we developed as children. If a child has experiences in which they feel neglected, abandoned or unloved, the feeling that "something must be wrong with me" can begin to develop. Why else would a child believe they aren't loved by the very people expected to love them unconditionally other than because "I must have done something wrong?" This can also occur if a child feels that they have to "earn" their parent's love. For example, when a child feels they are only loved or lovable when they get good grades or do all their chores. The moment they do something wrong they are filled with a feeling of shame believing that they are now "unlovable."

This relationship dynamic instills in the child a sense that, "I am not good enough" or "I am only lovable when I can do something for someone, and do it perfectly." These views of the self aren't developed only as a result of the child-parent relationship, they can also evolve from other sources or experiences we have while growing up. This feeling of "not being good enough" can also be seen as part of the human condition instilled in us through Adam and Eve and our "original sin." In the biblical story of Genesis[2], Adam and Eve are tempted to eat from the tree of "good and evil" thinking it will make them wiser and more like gods. When God searches for Adam in the garden after Adam ate the fruit, Adam hides saying: "I heard you in the garden; but I was afraid, because I was naked so I hid."[3]

Whether instilled in us through our "original sin," or developed through childhood wounds and experiences, it is our shame, insecurities and fear of being vulnerable or "naked" that keeps us from God. Once established, these false perceptions of self send us down a path of believing that nothing we do is good enough and that we are somehow incomplete. This state of disconnection leaves us searching externally for something to make us feel whole.

Without the skills and awareness to control our thoughts, the replaying of memories from past events can become all-consuming. Our obsessive repeating of what someone said to us, or the replaying of what we did and worrying about what other people may be thinking about us, keeps us deeply disconnected and discontent. Our unresolved feelings of guilt and shame carried over from our past are also a major component of our disconnection and ultimate discontent.

We often replay situations from our past over and over again in our head. As we replay these situations we activate emotions of shame, guilt, anger and insecurities that stir up the sense in us that "we are not good enough." It may sound absurd, but if we have the mindset that we are "not good enough" we end up constantly looking to remind ourselves that something is "wrong with us," because that is how our world makes sense. If we view ourselves as not being good enough and suddenly we start to succeed, then our world no longer makes sense. We will often choose a world that is unhealthy but familiar as opposed to a world that is healthier but unfamiliar. From a disconnected state, our lives become a cycle of reinforcing these negative views of our self.

These memories and our past experiences become our way of defining who we are. We convince ourselves that we are our emotions and experiences. This belief is reinforced as experiences and lessons get recreated, both in our memories as we replay past behaviors and in real time as we make the same "mistakes" over and over again.

The goal, which will be explored in more detail later in the book, is not to simply "forget" or "get over" past emotional and life experiences, but rather to bring forth an awareness of God that reminds us that we are not defined by our thoughts, experiences or emotions. We are defined and made whole through our relationship with God. Our reality is not shaped by our experiences and life circumstances, our reality is shaped by how we respond to our experiences and life circumstances. The goal is to respond from a God-centered space.

Desires and Attachments

As we move through life, our identity becomes connected with the many different roles we take on or are placed on us. As an infant, when we first recognize that there is an "I" and there is an "other," we begin to start formulating our definition of our "self." We begin to identify ourselves in relation to the objects and people around us. As each new role/title emerges in our life we begin to define ourselves by "what we do" (i.e. an athlete, musician, artist, our career, our work in the community, husband or wife, a parent). The list is endless. We end up replacing our "internal sense of self" (that which is defined by our intrinsic value and worth) with an "external sense of self" (that which is defined by what we experience, what we feel, what we think or what we have).

These roles are not unhealthy by their mere existence, they are made unhealthy by our illusion that they are what define us. When these roles are "who we are" rather than just "what we do" they become the perceived source of our self-worth and happiness. We become attached to them.

An attachment refers to the act of believing that our identity, happiness or self-worth are connected to external objects or conditions. It is the illusion that "This car will make me happy," or "I am valuable because of my job." This attachment to external roles and objects comes with an attachment to external praise and criticism. If we attach our self-worth to our job we will feel great when we get praised at work but feel terrible if someone criticizes our performance at work. This external element, our job, has been given complete control over our emotional state.

The illusion that our self-worth and emotional state are controlled by external factors keeps us detached from the present moment and disconnected from the presence of God. We spend our time looking externally for things that make us feel content or whole. This external searching often shapes how we search for God. We seek God externally but struggle to connect with the God that dwells within us.

Both God and our sense of contentment must be discovered internally. Before we can truly see God in the world we must be able to see God within ourselves. Before we can truly be content with the things in our life we must be content within ourselves.

Our external way of living creates a perpetual state of thinking that what we are looking for is always outside us. Our happiness and security are always at risk of being taken away, always just beyond our full grasp. We are fooled into the "I will be happy when…." way of thinking and living. The truth is, there is no "when." There is always something else that we think will make us a little happier or a little more secure: the bigger house, the newer car, the next promotion etc. If you can't be happy now, you won't be happy "then". Likewise, if you aren't able to see God in the present moment, you won't be able to see Him in any moment.

We live in a state of fear believing that our happiness and security are extremely fragile and could be stripped from us at any time. The fear of losing these conditions keeps us in a constant state of worrying about the future and obsessing over the past. When we get lost in our thoughts about the past or future, become swept up in our emotions or attached to external objects, we lose the ability to connect with the present moment. This disconnect ultimately leads to feelings of discontent—like something is missing.

In our projections about the future and our fixations on the past, we pretend to play the role of God. We decide what people say and do. We decide how people feel. We create a world in which we have complete control over each situation. God does not exist in the "reality" we project in our mind because that "reality" is not real. God exists entirely within God's own reality, the present moment. To leave the present moment is to leave the presence of God and venture off into a Godless world of our own creation. If you have ever wondered how things would feel in a world without God, just think about the last time you had a panic attack brought on by a situation you created entirely in your head. It would probably feel like that.

Through our thoughts and through our actions, we are quick to leave the present moment. Often afraid to embrace our difficult emotions or the pain we are feeling, we turn to behaviors that can mask them. This is a primary source of the addictions we experience and the root of our unhealthy behaviors. Afraid to embrace our whole-self, we live in the illusion of our disconnected-self. *Enough...*

Our disconnected-self is the "self" that only sees the parts of us that we want to see and doesn't acknowledge the painful and uncomfortable parts. Our disconnected-self is unable to fully recognize or appreciate our need for God. This disconnect pulls us away from the present moment and the presence of God.

We see how often we can get pulled into this way of living. However, there is another way of being. A way of being that connects us to the present moment and opens us up to the presence of God. This heightened state of awareness allows us to move beyond the illusion that our happiness and security exist outside of us and instead, we begin to reconnect with our whole-self.

Scriptural Reflection

Take time to read through this scripture. Read it slowly, at least three times. See if any word or phrase stands out to you. Think about how this scripture applies to your life today and how it is inviting you to transform.

"Therefore I tell you, do not be anxious about your life, what you will eat or what you will drink, nor about your body, what you will put on. Is not life more than food, and the body more than clothing? Look at the birds of the air: they neither sow nor reap nor gather into barns, and yet your heavenly Father feeds them. Are you not of more value than they? And which of you by being anxious can add a single hour to his span of life?

And why are you anxious about clothing? Consider the lilies of the field, how they grow: they neither toil nor spin, yet I tell you, even Solomon in all his glory was not arrayed like one of these. But if God so clothes the grass of the field, which today is alive and tomorrow is thrown into the oven, will he not much more clothe you, O you of little faith? Therefore do not be anxious, saying, 'What shall we eat?' or 'What shall we drink?' or 'What shall we wear?' For the Gentiles seek after all these things, and your heavenly Father knows that you need them all. But seek first the kingdom of God and his righteousness, and all these things will be added to you." (Matt. 6:25-33, ESV)

As my senses are coming back to life through mindfulness, I am becoming aware of the array of riches – sights, sounds, colors, movements, details – contained within every little thing and it's amazing.

Part II

Awareness of the

Present Moment

He knows.

Added... WHAT IS ESSENTIAL...?

I t is in the present moment that we relate and connect with the people and events around us and in turn, it is in the present moment that we can become open to connecting with God. Being aware of the present moment means we are aware of our inner self and exterior world. This awareness gives us the ability to choose how we can respond to situations rather than having an impulsive reaction based on our emotions and thoughts.

Our mind cannot be in two places at once, we cannot be consumed with mental projections about the future or stuck in our past, while also being attentive to how God is working in our life in the present. The belief that God is in all things and in all places at all times means He is present in each and every situation we experience, at the moment we experience it. When we fail to connect to what is happening around us and within us in the present moment, we fail to connect with God. By being fully present in each moment, experiencing each sight, sound, smell and texture, we are fully present to God. To intimately know the physical and emotional characteristics of the moment is to intimately know the physical and emotional presence of God. Let's first explore how to connect with the present moment so that we can then move deeper into connecting with the presence of God.

As we begin to explore the topic of meditation and eventually Contemplative Prayer, it is important to establish what we are referring to when we say "meditation" and "Contemplative Prayer" and how they differ. At the risk of oversimplifying, for this body of work, let us say that meditation is the practice of detaching from our thoughts and the external world and centering oneself with oneself. Contemplative Prayer is the practice of centering oneself with God. Contemplative Prayer is a practice of quieting the mind and opening our heart to the heart of God. Contemplative Prayer is a form of

Christian meditation. In this book, we focus on two popular techniques, Centering Prayer and Lectio Divina. Both approaches will be discussed in more detail later in the book.

Becoming Aware of our Thinking

Our thoughts are the greatest force pulling us from the present moment. To stay in the present moment we begin by learning how to be aware of our thoughts. Start by getting curious about your thoughts. Identify them, ask yourself: "Where did that thought come from? What made me think that? What does this thought tell me about how I am feeling right now?" You don't need to be afraid of your thoughts. You created them, the creator is always stronger than the created. Getting curious about your thoughts will help you uncover the deeper origin of what brought them on. The process of really digging into your thoughts should be done with the support of a trusted and professional guide, such as a therapist or spiritual director. Otherwise, you may find yourself just obsessing over your thoughts and not really getting to the root. There is a time and a place for everything, counseling allows you to explore and process things in a healthy safe setting. Meditation allows you to detach from being controlled by your thoughts.

Meditation

Growing up on Long Island I spent many summer days at Jones Beach State Park. I have a deep connection to the ocean. The ocean is in a constant state of motion, each gust of wind and change in the weather creates new conditions. Yet, with all this uncertainty, we can predict down to the minute the massive changes in tides. The ocean is the embodiment of action and stability. It has the power to change landscapes and reshape geography while the sounds of waves gently crashing along the shore can instill a deep sense of peace and serenity. It is a perfect metaphor for our own mind. ☺

I remember swimming out into the waves, and on days when the water was rough, as soon as one wave crashed overhead another one was right there behind it. It was always a mystery to me exactly where these waves were coming from, it seemed like one minute they weren't there and the next you could see water reaching up towards the sky as a new wave was suddenly approaching. Today I can find myself asking: "Where did that thought come from?" One minute it wasn't there and the next minute I can't seem to get it out of my head. On days when life seems extremely stormy, it can feel like as soon as I come up from one thought, another one is approaching to crash down upon me. yup.

I learned a valuable lesson growing up around the ocean. When you see a big wave coming, the worst thing you can do is turn and try to escape it. You'll never get to the shore in time and it always ends up crashing down on you and pulling you under. The best thing you can do is swim right through it. Take a breath, push forward and when you come up for air, the wave has passed over you and the water is calm. This is the meditation process. *Wow. I love that.*

The goal is to move through your thoughts until you find yourself "out past the waves." As you sit in meditation, thoughts will come. Some days they are big and frequent while on other days the waters of your mind appear calm and still. The waves are always strongest closest to the shore, so it is most challenging in the beginning to move beyond our thoughts; beyond the waves. With consistent practice and an ever-expanding internal openness, we soon find ourselves out past the waves — floating calmly on the water of our mind.

Brilliant analogy.

Within the meditation practice, it is a constant ebb and flow of detaching from our thoughts and getting pulled back into them. If we are not united with our point of focus (our breath, a mantra or sacred word), we can quickly find that we have been pulled back into the shore of our mind, back to feeling our thoughts crash down upon us. Unsure of how they were consumed by their thoughts again, it is common for people to describe the experience in the following way: "I felt relaxed and calm, and the next thing I know I had a thought about getting groceries, I wondered what I would have for dinner and suddenly I am thinking about how much money I spend a month on food and starting to feel anxious about my finances."

Growth and progress come with recognizing our thoughts and entering back into the water to begin again swimming out past the waves. Over time you will become more aware of the pull on your consciousness bringing you back to your thoughts. The way that we discover that we are not controlled by our thoughts is by discovering that we have the ability to acknowledge our thoughts and leave them behind as we come back to our single point of focus. If we are able to do this even one time, it is proof we can do it every time.

We must learn to be gentle with ourselves and not beat ourselves up over the fact that we were "thinking." Nor should we try to understand why we were "thinking" that thought. There is a time and place for "understanding why we think the way we do" or "why we feel the way we feel." However, the intention of our time in meditation is not to understand why but to accept what is. It is through acceptance that we learn to overcome.

It is in this acceptance that we learn to move beyond labeling something as a "positive" or "negative" thought. Each thought is treated the same — as a temporary sensation and a reminder to return to our breath. It doesn't matter if the thought is a memory of your best friend or something that reminds you of your sworn enemy, you should gently acknowledge it and return to your breath. This becomes the foundation for us to eventually move beyond attaching to and labeling thoughts, emotions or external experiences.

When an emotion or sensation stirs within us, we respond in the same way as when a thought pops into our head. We acknowledge it, and without judging or attempting to understand it in that moment, we gently return to our breath. As we discover that we can acknowledge and detach from an emotion, we begin to realize that, just as with our thoughts, we are not controlled by our emotions. This process helps us realize that just because we feel a certain emotion doesn't mean we have to act a certain way. As this practice builds within us, we are able to feel the emotions of shame, guilt, anger, etc. without having them control our behavior. This leads to eventually being able to "feel angry," process and move through the emotion and ultimately end up in a place in which you "act with compassion." This process will be discussed in more detail in the following section.

We are discovering that our thoughts and emotions do not control us but instead we can actually control our thoughts and our emotions based on how we choose to respond to them. This allows us to recognize that external events no longer have the power we once gave them. The co-worker or family member that you think is at fault when you get angry really isn't to blame at all. They simply acted a certain way that led to you having a thought, which led to you feeling an emotion which you chose to respond to with anger. Once you are aware that you control how you respond to your thoughts and emotions, you can understand that you can choose to respond in a different way. This doesn't mean that your co-worker or family member's behavior is respectful, kind or even appropriate, it simply means that you are choosing to respond to their behavior in a way other than with anger. You have now taken the power away from their actions. Meditation doesn't directly change the situations or "problems" in your life, or the way people in your life act. Meditation changes how you respond to the situations and people in your life. It is in our awareness that we control how we respond to life that we begin to experience true freedom.

So what does this meditation practice look like? It is a simple practice that can be extremely difficult. To avoid worrying about time, I suggest using a timer. Sit in a comfortable position with your feet flat on the ground and spine straight. If you are comfortable you can close your eyes, if not gaze softly down toward the ground. Place your hands on your stomach or in your lap, begin breathing in and out. Focus on the sensation of each breath — notice how it feels entering through your nose, feel it as it travels into your lungs. As you breathe in you should feel your stomach expand. Exhale. Feel your stomach deflate, notice the air as it travels out of your nose. Continue breathing in and out. Return to the sensation of your breath when you notice you have been thinking about something or feeling an emotion.

The act of thinking or identifying an emotion and then returning back to your breath is meditating. The warm, relaxed feeling we can sometimes experience once we have connected to our breath is a fruit of meditation, it is not actually meditation. Don't judge your meditation based on how it made you feel. Meditation is the practice, not the result of the practice. The goal is to sit down and stay true to the process of returning to your breath each time you find yourself distracted by a thought or emotion. If you do that for the full time allotted, you will have completed a "good" meditation session — regardless of whether you had constant thoughts the whole time or whether you were able to easily connect to your breath with hardly any thoughts. Any time you consent to sit still and practice is a "good" meditation session, any time you decide not to practice is a missed opportunity to grow.

Staying in the Present Moment

The practice of being in the present moment is about being aware of your thoughts, feelings and actions in the present. It brings us in direct contact with what we are thinking, feeling, doing and what is happening around us. It also allows us to understand how all four are connected.

Being fully aware of the present moment allows us to not think about the past or project into the future. Through meditation, we learn to be aware but not attached to our thoughts.

The process of becoming aware of the present moment allows us to identify our thoughts, process our emotions and then respond to the situation. First, we address what is happening inside of us, then we address the external situation. If a co-worker makes a comment to us that we feel is critical of our work our initial thought may be: "How dare they say that about me? Who do they think they are?" or "They are right, I am no good at my job." This thought can then trigger a feeling of anger towards the co-worker. This feeling of anger could then fuel our response to the co-worker.

If we are practiced in keeping our awareness in the present moment we will be able to recognize and identify this initial thought. Knowing that we are not defined by our thoughts or emotions we have the freedom to go deeper into our self rather than just remaining on the surface. As we drop deeper into our self we can discover the true source of our emotions. Perhaps the emotion of anger is really just masking a feeling of insecurity or shame. From this space, we can now focus on: "What can I do to address my insecurity? How can I become more confident?" rather than: "How can I release this anger out on my co-worker?"

It is important to note that we shouldn't be afraid to speak up for ourselves or speak our mind. The question is, what kind of mind are we speaking? An angry mind will speak anger. A peaceful mind will speak peace. It is about responding from a God-centered space rather than responding based on our thoughts or emotions. In this scenario, if your co-worker said something that was inappropriate or disrespectful, you should certainly speak up for yourself. However, the way in which you speak up for yourself should not be fueled by anger or insecurity, it should come from a place of empowerment and confidence. This process of identifying our thoughts and processing our emotions requires time and patience. The best thing we can do is not respond until we have completed this process. As you become more practiced in keeping your awareness in the present moment, you will be able to identify and process your thoughts and emotions quicker.

This process, coupled with the practice of Contemplative Prayer, allows us the ability to live in a God-centered space rather than a human, superficial space. Connecting with the present moment doesn't guarantee that you are then connected with the presence of God, but in order to connect with the presence of God, we must first discover how to connect with the present moment. As mentioned earlier, the present moment is a doorway to the presence of God, but we must intentionally walk through it.

Through His example, we can look to Jesus as a blueprint for how to live our lives and use His teaching as a guide to help us as we choose how to respond to situations. Through the Contemplative Prayer practice that is discussed later in the book, we develop a more intimate relationship with Jesus, allowing us to know Him more deeply and follow in His footsteps for living more clearly.

Common Roadblocks

There are common roadblocks that people experience when starting out in these practices. Acknowledging these hurdles will allow you to recognize them when they appear. Instead of running from them, learn to lean into them and see them for what they are: part of the process.

Whether we are discussing meditation or Contemplative Prayer, consistency in our practice is key. Contemplative Prayer and meditation need to be experienced and practiced. In the beginning, it doesn't need to be more than a few minutes each morning. It is just like exercising. Before you can run a marathon you need to run a mile, then five miles, slowly working your way up to 26 miles. We must set time aside to practice. Start with something small and gradually increase your time. It is more beneficial to do three minutes each morning than to do 20 minutes one day and then not meditate for another week. Consistency in practice will naturally lead you to wanting to spend longer periods of time in meditation.

On the surface, it may seem that starting with just minutes of our time each morning is simple. Yet, often people fail to consistently follow through and therefore are unable to progress. Let's take a look at some of the common roadblocks people encounter when it comes to prayer and meditation.

I am "too busy"

A common misconception in our society is that the more time we spend doing something, the more we will ultimately get done. This is false. What is true is that the more time we spend doing something from a healthy frame of mind, the more we are likely to get done. The 20 minutes I spend meditating in the morning and again in the evening are the most important activities I do all day in terms of helping me get my daily work done. No amount of responding to emails, texts or calls would make for a more productive day, or help me stay focused and on task, more than the time spent meditating.

Too often we multitask our prayer life. People often tell me that they pray all the time, "I pray while I drive" or "I talk to God throughout the day," and while that serves a role in our

I finally believe this

yes!

yup!

relationship with God, we need to care enough about ourselves and our time with God to be willing to set aside time in which we are not doing anything else and give our full attention to God. At its essence that is Contemplative Prayer, us giving our full attention to God. ✳

"My thoughts won't stop racing"

We are not used to sitting in silence and are unfamiliar with being still. The first step is to let go of the idea that meditation and Contemplative Prayer are immediately "relaxing." They aren't. At first, they are usually uncomfortable and at times terrifying. We are not accustomed to embracing silence and acknowledging our thoughts, without any means of distracting ourselves. As mentioned earlier, the remedy is not to judge your thoughts as "bad or good" but rather accept them as they are and gently return to your point of focus. Every thought is just another opportunity to return to the presence of God. This is a process and will take time. Be patient.

"I don't feel any difference"

Initially, the fruits of our prayer and meditation often take place under the surface and behind the scenes. It often isn't until we have been consistently practicing for a few months that something will happen and it will dawn on us: "I handled that differently than I would have six months ago." This practice is about being aware of our thoughts and emotions and moving beyond them. Don't worry if you don't feel anything happening, it is happening even when you don't feel it—trust in the process.

"I used to feel something and now I don't"

It is not uncommon for people to go through periods in which they don't feel the intensity or connection with God through prayer and meditation that they once did. This dryness or aridity[4], as it is sometimes referred to, is perfectly normal. St. Teresa of Avila, St. Teresa of Calcutta, St. John of the Cross, as well as many other lay people, have experienced extreme cases of this aridity. The main advice on how to handle this dryness is to continue with your prayer and meditation. Staying the course, regardless of how one is "temporarily feeling," is part of not being controlled by our thoughts or emotions. If we keep consistent with our practice, it will open us up to a deeper relationship with God. It is our way of confirming that our time in prayer is not just about "getting something." The goal is to consent to sit in God's presence — that alone is enough.

Having begun the work on connecting with ourselves and setting out to establish a consistent meditation practice to connect to the present moment, let's now delve into the third part of this book and process, connecting with the presence of God and Contemplative Prayer.

Scriptural Reflection

Take time to read through this scripture. Read it slowly, at least three times. See if any word or phrase stands out to you. Think about how this scripture applies to your life today and how it is inviting you to transform.

"God is our refuge and strength,

an ever-present help in distress.

Thus we do not fear, though earth be shaken,

And mountains quake at the depth of the sea,

through its waters rage and foam,

though the mountains totter at its surging. Selah

Come, and see the works of the LORD,

how he has done fearsome deeds on earth.

Who stops wars to the end of the earth;

he breaks the bow and splinters the spear,

he burns the shields with fire.

"Be still, and know that I am God.

I am exalted among the nations,

exalted in the earth!"

The LORD of hosts is with us;

Our stronghold is the God of Jacob

(Psalm 46:2-4, 9-12 NAB)

Lord...help me live this!
I am so sorry for my lack of trust!

Part III

Connecting to the Presence

of God

How we view ourselves is often how we view others and ultimately how we view God. Through the commandments, we are called to "Love your neighbor as yourself." However, if we don't love ourselves or think we are worthy of being loved, we haven't set a very high bar by which we can love our neighbor. Dorothy Day said: "I really only love God as much as the person I love the least." Oftentimes, the person we love the least is our self.

Contemplation, the fruit of Contemplative Prayer, is the pure and priceless gift of offering our whole-self to God. This offering of our whole-self requires a courageous level of trust. It requires having a personal and intimate relationship with God. We need to trust that we can expose our wounds to God and God will not use them against us, as may have happened in many of our human relationships. By becoming aware of our disconnect and the source of our discontent (part 1 of the book) and learning how to be aware and detached from our thoughts, emotions and experiences (part 2 of the book), we are now ready to invite God in to offer His healing. We are now ready to love our whole-self.

Our awareness allows us to be open about the pain, shame or guilt we feel regarding past or current situations. By building a personal relationship with God, we experience firsthand that God does not criticize or belittle us. Rather, we meet a gentle and loving God and realize that the negative judgments and harsh words were coming from within our own mind. As we continue to detach from our thoughts, we find God waiting there like the father welcoming home the prodigal son[5]. We encounter a God that loves us unconditionally. In the calm waters beyond the stormy waves of our self-judgment and criticisms, God is revealed to us to be the destination, the journey as well as fully present within us — the explorer. God is everything!

Redefining our Self-Worth and Identity through God

Now that we are open to the idea that we are not controlled or defined by what we think or feel or by external experiences in our life, we are left with the necessary question of what does define us? To continue down this path from a Christian perspective, we must at least be open to the idea that we are *divinely made:* we are made in God's image[6]. Even if you are at a point in your life where you can't possibly believe that this is true, I ask that you at least be open to the idea. After all, it is openness and willingness that are required, not belief. Belief is a fruit of openness and willingness, not a prerequisite.

To be made in God's image does not mean we are made without any room or need for growth.

It means that we are made with all the parts included. It means we don't have to search externally for any of our required pieces. I was recently in the store looking for a toy for my niece. I wanted to make sure she would be able to play with the toy that day, so I found a toy that said, "all parts included." There was no need to get additional parts or purchase batteries. The only thing we had to do was make sure we put the toy together correctly. This is our journey, learning how to put ourselves together correctly using all the parts of our self that have been part of us since birth. Unfortunately, many people are following a faulty set of directions. The fears and insecurities we cling to and allow to control us are not part of God's image. They are created in our mind and are not real.

At our birth, we are loved unconditionally and completely by God. Our value is at full capacity on day one, based entirely on something we had nothing to do with. As Fr. Richard Rohr puts it:

Another great analogy

"God doesn't love us because we are good, God loves us because God is good."[7] We are loved and worthy of God's love because God is our creator. That is the only requirement necessary and it includes EVERYONE! God's love for us is a constant presence in our life, it cannot be increased or decreased regardless of our life circumstances. We cannot earn God's love, it is bestowed upon us in full from the beginning. God doesn't love us more because we got a promotion at work and doesn't love us less if we are fired from work. His love for us is complete and therefore we are complete. For those that feel disconnected and discontent, not "whole" or not "good enough," the realization that we were created whole with no need to prove our self-worth changes everything. It is the epitome of freedom.

⟶ How can I live this?

Being aware of God's unconditional love for us and understanding that we cannot earn God's love is not a pass to do whatever you want. It is an invitation to draw closer to Him. When this invitation is answered, our lives become a reflection of God's love within us. We do not "do the right thing" in order to gain favor with God or even just because it is the "right thing to do." We do what God is calling us to do from within. We are made in God's image, our lives should be a reflection of His image within us.

The shift in perspective we need is beginning to see and define ourselves through God's eyes, rather than through our human eyes. When we see ourselves through the eyes of God, we recognize that our value comes from our Creator, not through our thoughts, emotions or deeds. If God doesn't use our thoughts, emotions or deeds to define us, then neither should we.

Explaining God's presence has to be done through metaphors and analogies, none of which come close to doing justice to the actual experience. I will do my best to make comparisons to everyday elements of our lives to help relate to God's presence.

God's presence is not dependent on anything we do. It is similar in a way to the race we belong to at birth. If you are born white, black or brown, none being better or worse than another, you remain that race throughout your entire life. No matter what happens during your lifetime, good times, hard times, successes or failures, your race does not change. You had no voice in deciding your race, you cannot change your race and even if you try to ignore your race, your race remains. Your race is constant throughout your life no matter what. God's love for us is constant throughout our lives no matter what. We are simply born into God's love. None of us had anything to do with "earning" it. There is no better or worse among God's children, we are all equally loved unconditionally.

Becoming God-Centered

To open oneself completely to God we must rid ourselves of the things inside us that block us from God. Our ego, shame, insecurities, fear and anger are perhaps the largest and strongest bricks in the internal wall we constructed to keep God (and other people) out. We must begin to lean into our pain rather than attempting to run from it. We can only give to God the parts of ourselves that we know and embrace and willingly hand over to Him. God doesn't take away our pain, He willingly accepts it once we present it to Him.

It is by identifying and accepting the "less attractive" parts of who we are and embracing our whole-self that we begin to deconstruct our human-self and connect with our God-centered self. By shining a light onto our areas of darkness we transform our pain by using it as a springboard to launch us deeper into the arms of God. We take the source of pain, open it, allow it to provide insight into "who we are and why we do what we do" and become transformed. This process creates a greater self-awareness of God's healing presence that exists within us. In the purest sense, self-awareness is God-awareness. It is by knowing ourselves that we can come to know God and it is by knowing God that we come to know ourselves. We are not God, but God is in us.

There are two things humans can bring to the Contemplative Prayer and meditation process: openness and willingness. The rest is up to God. Openness refers to fostering a curious and trusting heart to help us encounter the God that dwells within us. Our willingness refers to our practice of responding to God's invitation to dwell within us, which includes taking the time to sit in silent prayer and meditation each day. St. Teresa of Avila reminds us: "Since He doesn't force our will, He takes what we give Him; but He doesn't give Himself completely until we give ourselves completely."[8] To be completely connected with the presence of God is a process of "giving ourselves completely." In Luke 11:9, Jesus instructs us to "...Keep on seeking, and you will find. Keep on knocking, and the door will be opened to you." The challenge for all of us is to remain open and willing to keep on seeking and to keep on knocking. *Yes yes yes*

By remaining open and willing, God is revealed to us more and more. This revealing is a humbling process that helps us remove our ego and false images of self. This process is humbling because we encounter firsthand the awesome presence of God while acknowledging and accepting our own short comings.

We begin to let go or empty ourselves of our disconnected self." Self-emptying is the process of freeing ourselves from the illusions and lies we have internalized about our self that are rooted in our ego, shame, insecurities, fears and anger (i.e. I am not good enough). As well as detaching ourselves from being controlled by exterior attachments (including people, objects and events). We empty ourselves of all of the things that caused us to be disconnected. We do not empty ourselves and remain empty, we do it so that we may be filled with an greater awareness of God's presence. This is the process of going from our disconnected self to our whole-self. As we make room for God we are moved to continue emptying ourselves. Like a water wheel flowing into itself, by allowing God in we continue to be replenished with God.

Lord, I desire this to unfold within me.

Picture for a moment a scene in which you are trying to get to an appointment and the person in front of you is driving too slow. Frustrated, you find yourself becoming filled with anger. As your anger grows, the room for you to be aware of God's presence decreases. However, if you even decrease your anger from 100% to 90%, you now have made room for 10% of your emotional, mental and spiritual attention to become aware of God's presence. Increasing awareness of God's presence allows us to feel greater empathy for the other individual. The more you allow God's presence to fill you, the less anger you will feel regarding the situation. Bringing our anger down closer to 10% we can shift to thinking: "Perhaps the person is lost and needs to go slow to find their correct turn"; "Maybe I shouldn't drive so close to them, it is probably making them nervous"; "I too have been relaxed and in no rush before and have most likely been the person driving too slowly in front of someone in a rush" or "So what if I get there three minutes later? Will that really make a huge difference?" Any of these possibilities free us from the feeling of anger we once held. Instead of acting out of anger, we respond with compassion or empathy.

This process requires an awareness of the present moment (our thoughts, emotions and actions) and a relationship with God to help guide us to answer the question of, "How else can I respond?" Our response is not determined by some mere sense of moral responsibility to do the right thing. It is fueled by seeing the situation as an opportunity to reflect God's love in our life onto the world through our response to the situation. Every situation is, in fact, an opportunity to reflect God's love in our life onto the world.

Before we go into the fruits of Contemplative Prayer and being in the state of contemplation, let's first look at two forms of Contemplative Prayer: Centering Prayer and Lectio Divina.

Centering Prayer

Centering Prayer uses a sacred word or phrase as your anchor bringing your focus back to the presence of God. Your sacred word should be a word that brings to mind the presence of God, for example, "Jesus," "Holy Spirit," "Love" or "Peace." Any word or phrase can serve as your sacred word if it fits the description of bringing to mind the presence of God. Your sacred word can change from day to day but shouldn't change once you have started the meditation for that day. You don't want your mind actively creating new sacred words during the meditation.

Cool! Similar to how I adopted the practice of praying for a word of the day.

Our sacred word serves as a guide or anchor back to God. It is a reminder to turn our gaze back to Him when we get distracted. Ultimately the practice is to move beyond the sacred word, letting it go and resting entirely in God's presence. As we rest in His presence we will inevitably get pulled back to our human consciousness by thoughts, emotions or distractions. When this happens, we begin repeating the word again and following it back to the feet of Jesus. If you sit for Centering

Prayer and feel afterward that all you did was repeat your sacred word and think, that is fine. Remember not to judge yourself based on the "outcome" — it is all about the process.

Find a quiet place to sit, try to remove all outside distraction (i.e. turning off T.Vs, cell phones, computers etc.). I suggest setting a timer to avoid worrying about how long you have been praying. You can either have your sacred word picked out prior to coming to your meditation, or see what comes to mind once you sit down. Having established your sacred word for that meditation, sit in a comfortable position.

Now it is time to set your intention for the meditation. Your intention is essentially "to go to your own center, pass through that center into the center of God."[9] Setting the intention can be done by reciting a traditional prayer or by speaking a prayer from your heart. Our intention is not a "God gimme prayer", in which we ask God to do something for us. Our intention is focused on opening our heart to the presence of God, without any attachment to an end result.

Gently begin repeating your sacred word. I find it helpful to attach my sacred word to my breath. If it is a one-syllable word, say the word as you inhale, say the word as you exhale. If it is more than one syllable, say the first part on your inhale and the second part on your exhale. For example, I often use the phrase: "Jesus, fill me with your Holy Spirit," breathing in "Jesus, fill me with" and breathing out "your holy spirit." Each time we say our sacred word we should be reminded of God's presence. Instead of using a word you can also create a still frame image in your mind of Jesus to gaze upon (i.e. Jesus on the cross or Jesus standing on water). The image should be one still image and should not change during the meditation.

Our sacred word is our anchor connecting us back to the presence of God. When distractions set in — thoughts, emotions, outside noises — we gently bring our attention back to our sacred word, back to the presence of God. At the sound of the ending bell, we close with a prayer of gratitude and thanksgiving for the opportunity to sit in the presence of God.

Lectio Divina

Lectio Divina or "sacred reading" refers to the act of reading and meditating on scripture. Here is a common approach to Lectio Divina and the one that I use, both individually and in groups. Lectio Divina includes moments of reading (lectio), reflecting on (meditatio), responding to (oratio) and resting in God's presence (contemplatio).[10]

Again, just as in Centering Prayer, sit in a quiet place, try to remove all outside distraction and set a timer. Before beginning this process you should have a book selected and a passage picked out. I often use the gospel for the day, but you can use any passage you like, from any spiritual book that speaks to you. This process is meant to really help us delve deeper into the words, so I suggest not using a passage that is too long. It may become overwhelming and become hard to focus on a section.

Before reading the passage, start with a prayer to set your intention. This can be a traditional prayer that you recite or one spoken from your heart.

Read the passage three times. With each reading, we are striving to see how God is speaking to us through these words and to know Him deeper. The process of reading through the scripture is meant to engage our mind and spirit, not detach from it. We ask questions, we ponder meanings. Allow for a few moments of silence to reflect on the scripture after each reading.

During the first reading, we begin to open our heart to what is being said. We visualize what is happening. We can ask ourselves: "What is the overall message or theme being delivered in the reading?" Perhaps it's about forgiveness, love, inclusivity etc. We begin to become aware of any word or phrase in the reading that seems to touch us.

With the second reading, we look to uncover the message God is relaying to us through this passage. We ask ourselves: "What is taking place or being said in the scripture that I needed to hear today? How does this message apply to my life and what I am going through?" Again, looking to see if any word or phrase has jumped out at us. It could be the same word as in the first reading or it may be something new.

We then read the passage for a third time. After this reading, we ask, "How is God calling me to transform and grow through this reading? What do I need to change (do more of, or do less of) in my life based on this reading?"

Following the third reading and reflection, we enter into the meditation or contemplation stage. During the first parts of Lectio Divina, we were engaging our mind. In the contemplation phase, we are working to detach from our thoughts and outside distractions to open ourselves to God's presence. The purpose of the final part of Lectio Divina is to rest in the spirit of God. Using our breath, a word or phrase from the reading or one that relates to the reading (if the theme was about forgiveness you may want to use the word 'forgive,' even if that specific word was never actually used in the reading), gently begin repeating that phrase to yourself. At the sound of the timer, close with a prayer of gratitude for the opportunity to sit in God's presence.

Transcending our Suffering

Developing a relationship with God is like developing a relationship with a friend. It takes time, commitment and maintenance. By consistently sitting still in the silence of Contemplative Prayer and consenting to the process of becoming aware of God's presence, we become familiar with the soft, subtle language that God uses to speak to us. Think of when you spend time with a familiar friend; you know their facial expressions and mannerisms, the different tone of voice they use to express different emotions, you know what they are trying to say even if they don't know how to say it. This level of familiarity only comes after spending time really getting to know them. Being with an old friend also allows us to let down our guard and "be our self." We don't feel insecure or fear being judged.

The opposite is also true. How often do we meet someone new, and because we aren't familiar with them, interpret something they say the wrong way or completely misread a facial expression? Perhaps, out of fear of being misunderstood by someone that we just met, we don't fully speak our mind. If we want to know God, we must take the time to get to know Him. Contemplative Prayer allows us to become intimately familiar with God's language.

Consistent time in Contemplative Prayer means we don't only spend time with God in periods of crisis or distress. Too often we treat God as our "emergency plan" rather than taking the time to develop a real relationship. Too often we switch the roles and think that God is here to do what we want instead of understanding that we are here to discover what God wants. We turn to God in times of distress and then depending on the outcome either think "God answered my prayers" or "God abandoned me." Our trust in God is too often a conditional trust based on whether or not God does what we want.

Imagine if the only time a friend called you was when they needed your help. If you could help them they acted liked you were best friends and if you were unable to help them they wanted nothing to do with you. That would not be much of a relationship.

A deep and intimate relationship with God is not built on God answering our prayers but on seeing that God *is* the answer to our prayers. There is a contemporary Christian song by Natalie Grant with the chorus: "Help me want the healer more than the healing, help me want the savior more than the saving, help me want the giver more than the giving, help me want Jesus more than anything." [11] These lyrics beautifully describe a deep, intimate relationship with Jesus. Jesus instructs us to "seek first the kingdom of God and everything else will be provided for you." [12] This is the foundation of our relationship with God. The focus is on the blesser, not the blessings. We are able to identify and follow God's will more clearly when we remove our expectations about the outcome.) This requires trust and faith that we will not be abandoned by God. Our trust and faith grow deeper and stronger through consistent Contemplative Prayer practice. Building a relationship with God through consistent Contemplative Prayer allows the relationship to be strong and intact when we need to feel the support and protection that God provides us. When we need a friend to lean on, God is there.

After getting through a period of turmoil we often look back and see how God was with us throughout the experience. If we are willing to see it, we can usually acknowledge that the experience taught us a valuable life lesson, revealed to us a level of inner strength we didn't know we had, made us wiser, connected us with people that inspired us or brought us closer to God. After the storm is over and the pain has subsided, it can be easier to look back and recognize God's hand at work, but we don't have to wait until it is over before we remind ourselves that God is present.

If we have been consistently deepening our relationship with God through Contemplative Prayer, we will be prepared to see and feel His presence within our burdens, even as we are experiencing them. By recognizing that His presence was there with us in the past, we can trust that He is with us now as we go through our current pain. God doesn't change, so if it was true once for God, it is true always — God is with us in our times of darkness.

Our current pain is not just tragic life events, it includes our own inner work in which we confront our shortcomings and insecurities. As we empty out the space these shortcomings and insecurities once filled, we encounter the presence of God and we are given the grace-filled reminder that God helped us through this healing process. This reminder helps us continue moving forward, as we know with greater certainty that God is truly with us in our healing process. God's presence helps us as we work to remove these parts of our disconnected-self and as they are removed we encounter a deeper level of God's presence that exists within us. God's presence was instilled in us at birth but was covered over by our fears and insecurities to the point that we lost the ability to recognize it. The healing process is our ability to recognize God's presence once again.

The ability to see God in all things, even our pain and suffering, is the pathway to transcending our suffering and turning our burdens into blessings. This does not free us from human pain; what it does is give our human pain a divine purpose. This is on full display in Jesus' carrying of His cross. Jesus carrying his cross is the single greatest act of human pain and divine purpose. In the words of

Hebrews 12:2, "looking to Jesus, the founder and perfecter of our faith, who for the joy that was set before him endured the cross, despising the shame, and is seated at the right hand of the throne of God." The combination of embracing our human pain (our cross) while recognizing God's presence creates the deepest connection between man and God.

If every painful event, memory or emotion we are holding on to, or experiencing in real time, actually holds the key to unlocking a deeper, more intimate relationship with God, then all of these "burdens" are our roadmap to God and the ultimate blessing. The source of our pain becomes the source of our joy. It is our own ego, shame, insecurities and fear that block us from God. However, it is also our ego, shame, insecurities and fear that provide a pathway to a deeper encounter with God. With each self-realization about "who we are and why we do what we do", we clear out a little more of our human-nature within our soul, freeing up room for God to reveal His God-nature within us. God uses every part of us to help us know Him more.

Yes, Lord! Please!

We no longer need to be afraid to look at our self and instead we can lean into our own wounds. We invite God in to see every part of us because we know great healing and peace awaits us. We trust that God truly does "remove every branch that bears no fruit. And every branch that bears fruit he prunes to make it bear more fruit."[13]

Beyond the Present Moment to the Presence of God: Contemplation

Contemplative Prayer is the means by which we willingly consent to surrender our will to the will of God. It is through the silence and stillness of this prayer practice that we embrace the living God that dwells within us. The God that has chosen us to make his home in.[14] The state of contemplation is the fruit of Contemplative

Prayer and our willing consent to encounter God in the deepest darkest parts of our soul. These are the spaces we keep hidden from the rest of the world and, until recently, tried to keep hidden from ourselves. I say "until recently" because as we discussed earlier, we can only encounter God in the places of our soul that we have first been willing to go.

We bring our practice of not labeling our thoughts, emotions or experiences directly to our Contemplative Prayer practice. We remove any preconceived ideas about how God should respond to us, what God should do for us or what we should feel as a result of our prayer. Instead, we consent to the belief that to simply sit in God's presence is enough. We enter into prayer not in search of answers but to simply be still in His presence. It is in this stillness that God begins to take hold of our soul. Perhaps more accurately, it is in this stillness that we learn to let go of trying to be the one in control of our soul, which allows us to recognize that God does, in fact, have hold of our soul.

Jesus signifies the overcoming of the perceived separation between God and human. Through Jesus, we witness the potential for all humankind to become one with God. Through this unity, we are no longer controlled by our life circumstances or human emotions. Instead, we are guided by God's will, the divine presence alive within us. This indwelling becomes more apparent to us as we become more open to receiving it. Our openness to receive God is transformed from "theoretical" to "practical" through Contemplative Prayer. In the state of contemplation, we begin to "experience" God.

Our relationship with Jesus is made more real as we move from believing to knowing. This transformation is what allows us to move beyond our humanness into a God-centered way of living. Living completely in "human terms" we cannot escape the allure of "worldly things" (i.e. our thoughts, emotions, objects and events). Contemplative Prayer and the aligning of our will with Jesus' will enables us to hover above our own emotions and life circumstance. No longer controlled by what we think, what we feel or what is happening around us, we operate based on the intimate relationship we have developed with Jesus and the blueprint given to us through His life and death. This doesn't mean we don't feel the emotions or impact of the world, it means we no longer react based on those emotions or react based on the events of this world. Instead, we respond to our thoughts, emotions and the events of this world based on our intimate relationship with Jesus brought to fruition through our Contemplative Prayer practice. *Yes.*

In practical terms, we no longer have to "want" to do something in order to do it. We act based off of what God is calling us to do regardless of if we are in the mood to do it. This is true for meditating even when we don't want to, loving our neighbor even when we don't want to, to taking care of our self and going to the gym or eating healthy, even when we don't want to. We respond and live not based on our temporary human desires, but rather with a clear vision of the kind of life God has given us to live. Jesus reminds us that "the one who believes in me will also do the works that I do and, in fact, will do greater works than these."[15] Practicing Contemplative Prayer and experiencing the gift of contemplation, we live with the awareness that God is fully alive in us and is inviting us to be a reflection of His greatness for all to see.

Scriptural Reflection

Take time to read through this scripture. Read it slowly, at least three times. See if any word or phrase stands out to you. Think about how this scripture applies to your life today and how it is inviting you to transform.

"So then, my friends, because of God's great mercy to us I appeal to you: Offer yourselves as a living sacrifice to God, dedicated to His service and pleasing to Him. This is the true worship that you should offer. Do not conform yourselves to the standards of this world, but let God transform you inwardly by a complete change of your mind. Then you will be able to know the will of God — what is good and is pleasing to Him and

is perfect." (Romans 12:1-2, Good News

Translation)

Yes

Fiat!

yes.

Conclusion

The journey back to God, our healing process, occurs by walking through our pain, and discomfort. With courageous trust, we must walk into our darkness. If we do, we find that our darkness was nothing we had to fear. We find that our darkness is the pathway to our light.

Think about the last time you woke up from a nightmare, there was a moment when you realized everything that you were terrified of was never actually real. When you were asleep you were filled with fear, believing that what your mind was creating had the potential to actually harm you. Upon waking up, you realized that you were perfectly safe and that nothing that existed in your nightmare had any real way of harming you.

This is the peace we find in the presence of God. Awakening to God's love for us and His all-consuming presence in our life, we realize that we have nothing to fear. The pain from our past, the fears and insecurities that once controlled our every thought are unable to harm us. Our spiritual awakening is really just that, a waking up. We wake up from the illusion or nightmare of one world and realize a brand new reality. A reality that is filled with God's presence.

God's Presence in the Present Workshops

Michael Hoffner, LMSW currently leads God's Presence in the Present workshops. For a full list of upcoming events or to schedule a workshop near you please visit communitygrowthcenter.org/GPP

For mail correspondence:

P.O. Box 109

Port Jefferson Station, N.Y. 11776

About the Community Growth Center

The Community Growth Center is a non-profit holistic health center for self-discovery and contemplative healing located on Long Island, N.Y.

The Community Growth Center (CGC) combines the use of traditional and non-traditional social and therapeutic approaches. The CGC believes in giving individuals healthy food to eat, a creative environment to learn and a safe space to grow. Through the use of hands-on learning experiences, community involvement and compassionate guidance, the CGC is focused on providing participants with opportunities to grow in their mental, physical and spiritual wellness.

The Community Growth Center is committed to making sure that everybody, regardless of their financial circumstances, are able to access holistic health services. The Community Growth Center provides all of our services free of charge. We believe that financial hardships should never prevent individuals from receiving the care and compassion they deserve.

Learn more at CommunityGrowthCenter.org

Endnotes

[1] Thomas Keating, Centering Prayer: In Daily Life and Ministry, (New York, Continuum International Publishing Group, 1998), 17.

[2] Gen. 3, NAB

[3] Gen.3:10, NAB

[4] Brian Kolodiejchuk, Mother Teresa, Come Be My Light: The Private Writings of the "Saint of Calcutta",
(New York, Image Books, 2007)

[5] Luke 15:11-32, ESV

[6] Gen. 1:27, ESV

[7] Rohr, Richard. "Big-Love: Spirituality of Imperfection: Week 1." CAC.org. https://cac.org/spirituality-imperfection-week-1-summary-2016-07-23/ (accessed July 22, 2016)

[8] Kieran Kavanaugh, The Collected Works of St. Teresa of Avila. Volume 2 : The Way of Perfection (Washington D.C., ICS Publications, 2012)

[9] Basil Pennington, Centering Prayer: In Daily Life and Ministry, (New York, Continuum International Publishing Group, 1998), 10.

[10] "Lectio Divina." Contemplative Outreach. www.contemplativeoutreach.org (accessed April 19th, 2018)

[11] Grant, Natalie. Be One. Curb Records, 2015 MP3

[12] Matt. 6:33, NAB

[13] John 15:2, ESV

[14] John 14:23, ESV

[15] John 14:12, ESV

41609553R00073

Made in the USA
Middletown, DE
09 April 2019